MELODY & MEMORY

A POETIC EXPLORATION OF EXISTENCE

Madeleine Hornsby

Melody & Memory: A Poetic Exploration of Existence

© 2022 Madeleine Hornsby

Presentation by BookLeaf Publishing

Web: www.bookleafpub.com

E-mail: info@bookleafpub.com

ISBN: 9789358360806

First edition 2022

DEDICATION

This book is dedicated to Miley. Thank you for being my favourite
memory.

ACKNOWLEDGMENTS

I would like to start by acknowledging and thanking my photographer, Grace Ann, for her beautiful cover art. Thank you for being so dedicated to bringing my creative vision to life. I couldn't have asked for a more perfect cover photo for my first book! I would like to thank my family, friends and everyone who has made a significant impact on me during my life, be it for better or for worse. You have inspired many of these poems and, in many ways, shaped me into who I am today. If you recognise yourself among my pages and my words, know that I will always remember the reason I wrote them. I would specifically like to thank my parents. Some of my favourite poems in this anthology were inspired by memories of places we have travelled together. Thank you for providing me a culturally and geographically enriched childhood. Finally, my sincerest thanks goes to the team at BookLeaf Publishing. I am honoured to have had your support and guidance in publishing my first book and look forward to working with you again in the future.

PREFACE

Melody & Memory: A Poetic Exploration of Existence, tells the story of me. Through the melodic song-like nature of poetry I share with you my memories. Memories are curious and beautiful things. A persons' memories are likely the most unique thing about them and each individual memory moulds and shapes our lives. While it would be simply impossible to share all of my memories and life experiences, the best and worst of them have culminated into the writing of this book. The poems in this book detail the stories of people I have loved and lost, friends I grew up with, places I've travelled and experiences, both positive and negative, that have impacted my life. Another common theme that runs through the pages of this book, is art. Art in all forms has always been important to me and many of my memories involve all forms of art. From music to dance to visual arts and drama, an exploration of my life would not be complete without the arts. Although I share with you the personal occurrences of my life, like the lyrics of ones favourite song, I intend for these poems to be relatable. I hope that as readers, you might find yourself in the words of my poems and the pages of my book.

1. OUR MOON

The sky is my canvas.

Acrylics and ink

Sweep through the stars,

As I look up and think

Of you. It's been years

Since I've seen your face.

"Goodbye", and I flew

To a faraway place.

A bright, cloud-smudged moon

Rests her grand head

On the pillow of ink,

While words left unsaid

Circle my mind

Like rings round a planet.

It can't be much longer

now... Or, can it?

A pastiche of colours

Melt with the sun.

A sketch of the night

On the still horizon.

I wonder what time

It is where you are.

Do you see the moon,

Or the sun or the stars?

Our moon says she saw you

A few days ago.

Admiring her

In the afterglow.

For a moment the distance

Wanes and I smile.

United by art spanning

ten thousand miles.

On long, lonely days

I wait for nightfall.

Our moon reappears,

Stars echo her call.

"Do not be distressed

While you are apart.

You share the same moon,

The same sky, the same heart"

2. PEOPLE YOU KNOW

Childhood movies play

in an empty living room.

I visit when I get the chance

And nothing's changed.

The discs are simply older

(And a little worn out).

An old wardrobe stands

Centre stage, waiting

For its next victim.

I had always been suspicious

Of what lay behind

its shiny doors.

Delivered and opened

Without a response.

A once crisply folded

Letter lays tattered

On the doorstep.

I never got one back.

Familiar echoes murmur

In the hallway.

Pop punk music blasts

From a pink CD player.

It's chaotically loud, but please,

Don't change the volume.

Golden sunshine seeps

Into the farmers' fields.

The heat can be harsh,

But it's good for the flowers.

A wise, old friend

Helps the sugar cane grow.

Heavy brushstrokes

On a timber door drip

Down grooves like tears.

The pigment fades quickly

After it dries.

I don't repaint it.

Identical chairs sit

On opposite sides of a dining

Table. Time and overuse

Distresses the leather.

A seam finally tears.

The beloved chair is thrown out.

Jade coloured curtains

Kiss the musty floor.

Nonchalant and unassuming

I hardly notice they're there.

Occasionally I draw them back,

But they usually stay closed.

Mirrored glass atop an

Antique desk. A tiny crack

lingers in the corner.

The dressing table is elegant,

But everyone points out

It's flaw.

Metallic lights hang

From the tall ceilings.

Bright yet understated,

They are home to a colony

Of cobwebs. Even if I don't

Turn them on, I know they still work.

Oil upon a white canvas.

I took it off the wall recently.

Beautiful paintings look different

Under bright lights.

I realised I don't like it

Anymore.

"Zodiac Diary -2018" rests

on a nightstand. Untouched

For years, with a broken spine.

The keeper of many wasted,

worthless memories

That I wish I could forget.

3. GAS LIGHT

At the fall of dusk

She stalks the streets.

Gold hair and doe eyes

Deceive those she meets.

The lamplighter's daughter

Looks sweet from afar.

But, her temper is gruesome.

Her presence, bizarre.

She's selfish and greedy,

As vain as they come.

Heartless and cruel,

Her soul? Well, it's numb.

Wielding her wick

She paces the park,

Lighting each lamp

To escape from the dark.

Flames burn behind her,

All in a row.

At the end of the path

There is one lamp to go.

The last lamp is different,

Tall and antique.

Embellished in gold,

It is shiny and sleek

But this lamp is broken,

It should not be lit.

This makes the girl angry

And so she commits

A crime. An arson

Attack in the dark.

Gasoline doused

On the lamp in the park.

Tossing her wick

Into the thick oil,

Red blazes erupt

As the lamp starts to boil.

She watches the fire

Until she is sure

Her violent destruction
Will finish with gore.

Remorse is not felt

For the dainty, gold light.

She tosses her hair

And stalks into the night.

The lamp is left burning,

Consumed by thick flame.

It's glass windows melted,

Deformed and in pain.

The smell of smoke wafts

Down the dimly lit lane.

The little girl smirks

She is proud (and insane),

For she feeds on the wreckage

As she turns her back.

A criminal with hints of

Pyromaniac.

The fire subsides

As dawn reigns upon

The dewdrops, and fog

Floats like dainty chiffon

On the ash covered grass.

Below the burnt light,

Park goers gather

Around this new sight.

For the lamp is not damaged

But, she is unique.

An artwork formed from

A stunning antique.

Each day hundreds come

To admire the light,

Twisted and curled

And glowing. Despite

The vengeful attack

Of a few days ago,

The lamp now burns brighter

And pink flowers grow

Up the gold light.

They wrap round burnt glass,

As admirers sit

Upon the park grass.

"And the girl?" You ask.

Well, she was not heard

From again. But she'll pay

For the trouble she stirred.

4. LIFE IMITATES ART

A pencil dances

Across a sheet of paper,

The tip of the lead

Embracing each cellulose fibre

As it pirouettes between them.

Glossy paint oozes into

Each crease, filling the page

With life. Layer upon layer,

Individual shades harmonise

Like a colourful choir.

Graphite shading erupts

Dramatically on the crisp,

White paper, detailed

And expressive as

A Shakespearean soliloquy.

As ink begins to flow,

Highlights and shadows

Emerge poetically from the page.

This artwork recounts the stories

Of a hundred novels.

5. WINTER REUNION

Wind and sunshine meet

At the park in the city,

Dancing through bare trees.

6. COMPLICATED

My saviour complex keeps

Telling me I can change you, but

Years of patriarchal conditioning

Aren't so easily undone.

I can't tell if you see me

As a "friend" or an object

You crave control over.

Either way, I can't play

Our game by your rules.

You are my weakness.

An addictive poison I can't

Seem to stay away from.

We're like fire. Dangerous,

Yet somehow beautiful...

Until everything burns down.

Your fiery ego ignites me,

Blanketing me in thick, warm ash.

You assume I will submit

To your manipulative tongue,

But my stubbornness proves

A worthy opponent on our

Treacherous battlefield.

I still don't understand

Why you left me.

Perhaps you felt vulnerable

Tangled in my charm.

Whatever the reason, thank you.

Thank you for letting

Me go, so I may grow.

I want to hate you, I really do.

But, somewhere deep down,

I hope I never lose you.

7. YOU HAVE THE RIGHT TO BE SCARED

November 3rd, 2020.

Anticipation lurks like a shadow in the night.

It feels like Christmas Eve, bubbling

Not with excitement, but with fear.

My country will descend into anarchy.

They've bordered up shop fronts.

They're urging vulnerable minorities to protect themselves.

I call my friends. Please be safe.

Maps flash red and blue and red and blue,

As swingers teeter on the edge

Of humanity and autocracy.

I assure myself I've done all I can.

Reality slips further into the realm

Of dystopian fiction. The people are rioting.

If not now, they will be tomorrow.

When the war began.

2:20am. I can't sleep.

I have the right to be scared.

We all do. Whether you hold

The eagle crested leather or not.

"Raise a glass to freedom.

Something they can never take away"?

The Land of the Free dipped it's toe

In the violent waters of authoritarianism.

The impending events are unpredictable,

but if life intimates art,

Colour theory states

That BLUE neutralises orange.

8. GLITTER IN THEIR VEINS

Legend says "some girls are born

With glitter in their veins".

Paparazzi start to scorn

While she injects cocaine.

Glitter drips down canvases

And fumes of spray paint waft,

Like the scent of cannabis

Polluted lungs did cough.

Psychedelic pink and gold

Obstructs the gloomy prints.

A reckless vehicle uncontrolled,

Driven under the influence.

November third in Cleveland,

A defiant fist was raised.

Feminism in command.

Mugshot forever praised.

Powdered plastic dipped in rose

Upon a white facade.

Riot guns, the violence grows

Into a prison charge.

Hollywood imprisonment

Is always well observed.

Handcuffed for their ill intent?

Poetic justice served.

*The above poem is inspired by Scott Redford's series of artworks, entitled Reinhardt Dammn: U Could B Mine (2010) .

9. OVER-CAUTIOUS DAYDREAMER

Eyelids flutter like butterflies. She's awake.

Relief is subverted by intrusive thoughts.

Daydreams ravage her mind.

Rephrase: nightmares. Day nightmares.

A debilitating cycle of "what if".

Do you believe in the butterfly effect?

She does. The dreaded panic ensues.

Anxiety's grip tightens around her throat.

She leaves the house. What if ...?

The door clicks shut.

1234   5678

There was a fire today did you hear?

Old house, near the cinema.

The nightmares tussle for power over logic.

Golden flames entrap

Her battered mind,

While butterflies writhe in her stomach.

Taken hostage by her brain,

It sabotages her body's ability to function.

An intruder lacerates her thoughts.

Desperation for control

Compels her to madness.

1234   5678

Caution tugs on her puppet strings,

Prohibiting every small risk.

She surrenders to the flood-like thoughts.

Compulsions should be the lifeboat,

But an anchor lurks below.

It drags her further into the abyss.

Home is shrouded in familiarity.

Routines spiral over time.

Trapped like a butterfly in its cocoon house,

Longing for certainty.

Kitchen tiles.

1234   5678

678

7

8

10. VILLAIN

You clutch a thin brush

And soak it in ink,

Painting me as the villain.

Your wickedness slinks

Like a snake in the night

Past the people you know.

They think you're sweet

If only you'd show

Them the girl you showed me,

When you finally snapped.

Insecurity provoking

A violent attack.

You called me "unstable".

Words sharp as a knife

Stabbed at my back

As you slaughtered a life's

Worth of friendship. I know

Now that you never cared,

And I hope I forget

All the memories we shared.

11. SALZBURG COTTAGE

In a tiny cottage

Wrapped in vine,

A parcel sits

Tied up in twine.

A copper kettle

On the stove

Whistles, as the

Children wove

Mittens of wool

By the fireplace.

Satin blue sashes

Tied round white lace,

Their dresses were dainty,

Handmade with love,

From recycled curtains

That once hung above.

Snowflakes fall gently,

They melt into spring

And settle on roses,

Raindrops glistening.

Music erupts from

The house on the hill,

While golden sun settles

Upon the window sill.

12. ABANDONED

Crystal chandeliers

Rust, as cobwebs weave around

Unopened windows.

Decaying floorboards

Creak no more. Phantom footsteps

Precede illusory

Shadows.

13. MIXED

Harsh sunlight nudges it's way

Through dense black cloud.

Blinding iridescence ruptures

The pale sky, but is quickly

Swallowed by the fog.

The city is dreary and cold.

An obnoxious, theatrical flash mob doused

In sequins, attacks the lifeless square

and disappears as quickly as it came.

Silence suffocates the town once more.

A high speed train rattles

Violently over rusting tracks.

Momentum swells as the carriage

Begins to swing. The screech of

The brakes is haunting.

Crackling flames folic peacefully in the

Fireplace. A curious spark escapes

Setting curtains and carpet ablaze.

The quaint cottage surrenders

To the ravenous inferno.

How quickly everything has changed.

14. SUMMER LOVE

I fell in love three summers ago.

Not with a person,

But with a place.

English Gothic towers ornamented

With Cherubim, climb toward

A bright blue sky, while

Punters heave their poles

Through the shimmering stream

Below. Academia blossoms

Like spring flowers in the

College courtyards,

As eager students seek solace

In shadowed cloisters.

My friends and I indulge

In iced tea and ice cream

In between our classes.

Each of us, though far from home,

Feels comfortable in the city.

Our campus quarters embraces us

Like a long lost friend.

Familiarity winds up every staircase

And skips down each hallway.

The Christ Church clock tower

Strikes eight o'clock.

The dining hall and its portrait patrons

Welcome their guests.

Outside, Palladian principles

Carved in stone, dominate

The skyline. Fairy tale streets

Come alive as fauns and lions

Frolic under magnolia trees.

Lampposts dimming from the

Night before, stand proudly

On the corners of cobblestone lanes.

I long to reunite with my lost love.

To sip elderflower lemonade

And watch Shakespeare in the park

On a midsummers eve.

History and culture honeymoon

In Oxford, their marriage breathing

Life into each delicately sculpted

Turret and perfectly moulded pillar.

No matter how far I stray,

My heart and soul belong here.

I ask the city to keep my memories

Safe until I return.

15. MEMORY LANE

On memory lane,

My footprints grow, as the path

Winds delicately toward the present.

Tiny, baby feet begin to imprint

The concrete upon the creation of

The trail. The scenery is blank.

I have no memories that stretch so far

Back. Perhaps we may borrow some

From my mother or father's lane.

My path swims across oceans

And darts rapidly between

Continents. Indentations of winter boots

Are replaced with sandy footprints.

The soles of school shoes

Frequent the growing lane,

As memories begin to appear.

Down my lane there is music.

There is dancing and singing and art.

Flag bunting zig-zags overhead.

The flags of beautiful countries woven

Together and strung in the forefront

Of my memory. Texts book are

Piled on the side of my footpath,

Stacked so high they might soon

Topple over. At every anniversary

Marker, handmade birthday invitations

Inhabit little gold mail boxes

And the smell of cake and chocolate

Drifts on the April Breeze.

Not long ago, the lane turned grey.

A heavy fog still hangs over those memories

Asphyxiating even the pleasant ones.

Unsightly evils loom in the dangerous abyss.

Signs plastered on the side of the

Footpath, read "WRONG WAY, TURN BACK".

But a traveller must conquer the darkness

If she is to find the purest light.

My lane is imbedded with the footprints

(And paw prints) of those who have

Walked beside me. Their names

Are carved in the concrete flooring,

And embellished with shiny paint.

Some lost, but none forgotten,

Each of them have earned

A permanent place

Down my memory lane.

16. THE BOOK SHOP

On the high street stands

An old book shop.

A rickety door

With a bell on top,

Invites its guests

Into a world

Where life resides

On pages curled.

The old wood door

Creaks in tune

To sounds of readers

Pacing, soon

To find the book

That seems to leap

Off its shelf.

It's theirs to keep.

Organised by

Name and theme,

The bookshop shelves

Concoct a scheme

To capture readers

Like a maze

Of vibrant verses

In a daydream haze.

The shop is home

To friends we know,

Like Amy March

And her sister, Jo.

Among the dust,

They laugh and jest

Admired by

Each book shop guest.

Despite its old age

And rickety door,

A magic is present

Inside the book store,

For it opens a gate

To wondrous lands

And poignant ideas,

Both thrilling and grand.

17. BITTERSWEET ARCHIVE

Somewhere in mind,

There's a chamber.

A chest bound under

Lock and key

That holds the

Outcasts of my

Memory.

I call it,

The Bittersweet Archive.

Memories of all multitudes

Are kept here.

Thoughts of places

I spent a lot of time in

But never really liked,

Are bundled away in my archive.

The sheet music for

Every song I've ever performed

Is filed alphabetically

Inside the chest.

But mostly, it is filled with

People.

Friends I shared

So much of my life with,

Yet haven't spoken to

In months. The Archive

Stores and protects

Our memories.

These are memories that

I never want to lose,

But don't particularly want to remember.

Memories I once treasured,

And now refuse to think about.

Memories of friends that I

Used to call my sisters.

Now, I don't know anything

About them.

Just like a junk draw

In a kitchen, I think

Everyone should have

An Archive.

A little corner of one's mind

Where you can store

Things you can't quite

Bring yourself to throw out,

But will never use again.

This way, there is space

For new memories,

And my mind isn't

Cluttered with useless

Kitchen utensils.

18. AMRON

The Queens portrait hangs outside the pub,

Blowing gently in the British breeze.

The smell of fish and chips

Floats on crisp, cold air.

The corner shop is bustling

With frosty hands clutching at

Cups of coffee and hot chocolate.

Across the highway,

Tiny chairs and tables line

The window of an old shop front.

Delicate fingers examine

Miniature books and tiny kettles,

While fur trimmed coats pile

Into the bakery next door.

Two sausage rolls with tomato sauce

Please, and a cheese scone.

I tread lightly along the lane of stars.

A black cat purrs at my feet

And follows me home.

As I open the door, he slinks

Into the neighbour's garden.

This little village and I are old friends.

19. M

I feel your presence with me

Although you're far away.

Our last goodbye a year ago,

I miss you every day.

I have a small initial

Tattooed on my wrist

To keep you close beside me.

I begged and prayed and wished

That you might wake up again

That night you went to sleep.

I placed your paw into my palm.

My eyes forever weep.

When I cannot stand the pain

I look to my tattoo,

Inked forever in my skin

Reminding me of you.

20. THE END

The end is often

Bittersweet.

A new beginning dawns

Upon the pages

Of this book

And memories we mourn.

We leave behind

What we once knew

And take what we have learnt,

For endings melt

To souvenirs,

Like wax from candles burnt.

A sun that sets

Upon the shore,

A final chord of song,

Are necessary endings

Placed in spells

We shan't prolong.

While music played,

The light did fade

Into a gentle hue

Of purple first,

Then black and blue

And you

Went with it too.

www.ingramcontent.com/pod-product-compliance
Lightning Source LLC
Chambersburg PA
CBHW072049150726
47996CB00015B/2320